Belief and Ethos

NEHEMY N.KIHARA

DEDICATION

Dedicated to all the nomadic pastoralists, cultivating farming and

working communities of Laikipia , Great Rift Valley,

Beyond Mount Kenya, and all over the World.

.Whose everyday life is guided by belief on the Almighty Creator of

the ever-present day light giving sun and occasionally visible moon,

the plants that feed humanity and animals.

Dedicated to all those whose ethos, and world view of

the planet, mother Earth and Universe is about the interconnected

web of the Divine, Nature and Humanity.

.

CONTENTS

ACKNOWLEDGMENTS

To my Psychological /Symbolic Anthropology Professor and
Advisor Dr .Robert Paul then Chair
[Department of Anthropology-Emory University]
-currently in private Psychoanalysis practice and
teaching Anthropology / Department of Psychiatry,
My Social Psychology Professor Linda Molm, then Chair
[Department of Sociology -Emory University-] currently
teaching at University of Arizona
The late Dr. Earl Brewer , my Sociology of Everyday Life Professor
My public service and academia life is indebted to their
teaching and research contributions

1 INTRODUCTION

This book seeks to examine the socialization process in terms of:-

1. Development of the personality and its transformation

2. The acquisition of acceptable behavior patterns (culture)

3. Human survival, interdependence and discipline (moral precepts).On one hand the paper will seek to examine the socialization process in relation to culture and personality.

While on the other hand critically examine the religious perspectives in this relationships in an ever changing social situation and everyday living.

The book seeks to argue that any attempt to ignore or totally exclude religious perspectives from culture and personality studies is not only unnecessary but weakens the whole field of psychological anthropology.

Therefore in conclusion, it will be argued that:-

1. Religion (especially values and norms) is an internal part of the socialization process and thus a part of culture and personality. (Psychological Anthropology).

2. Thus, it should be given the serious consideration it deserves, without necessarily attempting to explain it away as a mere illusion of the human culture and personality.

3. The psychological anthropological perspective is useful in the study of the religious phenomena.

2 PSYCHOLOGICAL ANTHROPOLOGY

If one had to think of the field of Anthropology strictly as the study of human species, namely the cultural aspect. One can divide it into four major areas: Socio-cultural, Archeology, Linguistics and Physical Anthropology.

However, the book deals specifically with the area of culture and personality or psychological anthropology. While most studies falls in the areas of cross-cultural study of cognition and transcultural psychiatry this book seeks to examine a third and central aspect of culture and personality.

3 CULTURE

Central to the science of Social or Cultural Anthropology is the concept of culture. The main problem is the understanding of this concept. To some anthropologists it is a learned behavior while to others is not, yet to others it exists in material objects.

On the earliest definition of culture is found in E.B. Tylor (1871:1)Primitive Culture; "Culture is that complex whole which include knowledge, believe, arts, morals, laws, custom, and any other capabilities and habits acquired by man (woman) as a member of society". The Tyrolian conception of culture equates it to thing and events that are particularly honest - artifacts and techniques.

This was a view that was supported by Robert H. Lowe's(1920), Primitive Society .

However Kroeber and Kluckhohn (1952:155'169) in Culture: A Critical Review of Concepts and History; said that "Culture is an abstraction from the concrete behavior, but, it is not itself behavior The later view is supported by Beals and Hoijer in their statement that an anthropologist cannot observed culture directly; since it cannot be seen as, we can the individuals, their actions and interactions.

Much of this debate centers on the concern with distinction between culture and human behaviour or with views like Felix M. Keesing's (1958; 16) Cultural Anthropology. Culture is "the totality of learned, socially transmitted behaviour."

Other anthropologists deal with the question at length without coming to an agreement of what they mean by their concepts. Ralph Linton (1936:363) question the existence of culture at all.

In almost the same the thought Redcliffe-Brown (1940:2) says that the term culture is an argued abstraction with no concrete reality, and Spiro (1951:24) supports the same view by saying further that this abstract has no ontological reality.

One thing that is clear in the struggle to define culture either as behaviour or abstraction from behaviour is that this is in proper the central problem of Cultural Anthropology - as it seeks to understand its boundary with psychology i.e. anthropologists attempting to define their subject matter without necessarily psychologizing.

In the midst of this Leslie A. White (1940) "the symbol: the basis of human behavior, the philosophy attempts an analysis to distinguish between psychology (study of behavior and anthropology (Culturology) as the study of Culture.

This theory examines the possibility of considering things (objects) and events (acts) and their dependence upon symbolling (symbolates) these may be interpreted first in terms of their relationship to human organisms; (i.e. in somatic context) and secondly, in terms of their relationship to other things and events (i.e. in an extrasomatic context).

By "symbolling" the anthropologist means bestowing of meaning upon a thing or an act; or grasping and appreciating meaning thus bestowed.

Culture, then, is a class of things and events, depend upon symbolling considered within an extrasometic context. It is therefore real and existing in space and time, within human organism (concepts, beliefs, emotions and attitudes, within process of social interaction among human beings and within material objects lying outside human organisms but within patterns of social interaction (Sapir (1932:236).

According to White, therefore, culture is thus intraorganismal, interorganismal and extraorganismal. Every cultural element has a subjective and objective aspect. a thing is subjective since it has a concept and an attitude on the other hand a concept or an attitude is objective since it has an overt expression in speech behaviour.

(Leslie White's) the locus of culture.

 (1) Ideas and Attitudes

(2)   Overt acts

(3)   Material Objects

The three symbolates culture.

0 - Persons

* - Objects - and lines of interaction or interrelationship

This sort of view was presented in this paper because it defines the distinction put by some people like Leslie White to show of the scientific basis of studying culture as connected actually in logical (scientific analysis) with this view in mind

Sapir (1932:233) that culture cannot be realistically disconnected from those organizations of ideas and feelings which constitute the individual. And this leads us to other level of Psychological Anthropology - i.e. personality.

4 PERSONALITY

Even with a definition of culture like the one held by Leslie White so, well scientifically grounded-culture includes a personality component.

Boas (1928:236) tells us that the forces that bring about the changes are active in the individuals composing the social group, not in the abstract culture.

Malinowski (1941:73) state that a "cultural fact starts when an individual interest becomes transferred into public, common and transferable systems of organized endeavor: Linton (1936:274) things becomes cultural when it has been transmitted to and shared by one other individual in the society.

This idea is supported Durkheim (1938:I:V) while these may be unsatisfactory explanations of culture by some, they indeed for the purpose of this paper point to the fact personality structure comes into the picture in that culture does not exist a part from both the idea and the real, the subjective and objective. Hallowell (1945:175) in one way gives one side of the picture and yet a true one, when he says that in a literal sense cultures never have met nor will ever meet.

What is meant is that people meet and that, as a result of the processes of social interaction, acculturation - modifications in the mode of life of one or both peoples may take place. Individuals are the dynamic centers of this process of interaction.

This view is true in that culture does not exist independently of people nor do people exit without a culture. One might further say that people's behavior is a response to, a function of, their culture. Which is the independent and which the dependent variable is - culture or behaviour still remains a point of debate.

Herskovits (1948:28), also to some not clear in his statement, says that when culture is closely analyzed, we find but a series of reactions that characterize the behaviour of the individuals who constitute a given group. Leslie White rejects individual and psychological explanation in favor of an explanation of human behaviour through the super-organic.

However, his rejection of such an approach far from not being useful to Psychological Anthropology; seems to me to be useful in balancing any extreme reductionism that the non-revolutionary, noncomparative and non biological theorist might attempt to follow.

Moreover his cultural evolution is more useful when contrasted with such theories as Ruth Benedict's (1934:46) who says that "a culture, like an individual, is more or less consistent pattern of thought and action. Within each culture, there come into being characteristic purposes not necessarily shared by other types of society.

Coffman (1961:142) in whose view society understands the individual as a multiple-role-performer rather than a person with a particular role and hence a person of many identifications.

On one hand the expectations of which individuals comfort with moral expectations of the culture will determine the nature of social encounters.

LeVine (1973) on the other hand argues for a distinction between behaviour which conforms with cultural expectations and the inner experience which disposes the individual to behave in certain ways. Gardner Murphy (1947) suggests that personality may be viewed as a theoretical construct contracting three levels of complexity: it may be seen as an individual, as a structured whole, or as a field consisting organism and environment.

However, personality also include the dimension of culture this raise the need and necessity of systematically examining all human behaviour within the context of cultural determinants the necessarily controlled variables (if Goltschalk, Klockholm, Angel., 1945). Kluckholm, 1940; Malinwiski, 1935, Mead, 1947; Whiting and Whiting 1960).

Personality structure are thus learned patterns dependent on cultural environment, but they are not more reliable to analysis only in cultural terms than cultural terms are reducible to psychological patterns.

In conclusion, we can say that we have considered various working definition of culture and personality. At least we have seen the background of a distinct theoretical orientation called Psychological Anthropology. This evolves around theoretical framework applicable to the study of human behaviour as determined both by cultural and personality variables.

In his "mazeway" theory Wallace (1961) suggested that mutual predictability of behaviour is more important in understanding the operation of social structure than actual shared motives.

The approach by Phillips and Wallace tends to move away from the more static and culture deterministic aspects of the configurationist theories.

The assumption, therefore, is that in performing roles people can behave in the same way from different motivational base. Both psychological mechanism of internationalization and the nature of moral development induces and orients behaviour within a culture, This cannot be separated from the nature of role expectations as they influence the structuring of behaviour in any culture.

Barry, Bacon and Child (1957) found that in a majority of societies girls experience generally greater pressure toward taking nurturing attitude, toward obedience and toward responsibility. Boys were more influenced toward self-reliance and achievement activity. They reported notable differences in roles of men and women related to economic functions in society.

Frazier (1940) and Cohen (1955) describe the effects of slavery of in Black families, especially the absence of the father.

Boyer (1964) studies the maliforcelity in (native) Indian American cultures, while Glokman (1954) and Levine (1961) discuss retrailized customs in African cultures relating either to political hostility or to antagonism between the sexes. In other words these note role reversals which may lie in cross sex identification and a desire to take one some of the aspects of the opposite gender

5 SOCIALIZATION PROCESS

In the field of `Psychological Anthropology' the process of socialization is considered in the influence of culturally determined child rearing practices, role expectations, and values or intellectual and emotional development as well as the general socialization of the individual.

Child-Rearing:- The psychological theories of psychoanalysis and learning lay much emphasis on the fact that early childhood experiences are determinants of patterns of adult behaviour. Kardiner's concept of "basic" personality is one of the approaches in anthropological.

Studies which in addition to from Mead (1928, 1930) challenge the assumptions about the universality of adolescence as a period of strife or of latency period as a period of lack of sexual knowledge.

His theory emphasized that each society has a basic way of conditioning early experiences so as to produce similar configurations in adult personality among its members. The `primary' social institutions are the family and economy in which the child receives early socialization. The secondary social institutions of a culture discerns basic personality structure which rises from the primary institutionalized social behaviour.

The secondary institutions are the expressive patterns in cultural behaviour found in folklore and religion. In every culture therefore, there are a number of deviants from the basic personality pattern of that culture.

Linton, (1945) uses the concept of modal personality to emphasize the fact of modalities of behaviour found within a society. Wallace (1952) extends this in terms of personality types in the anticipation of more than one given pattern of modal for a group.

Bateson and Mead (1942) with their graphical monographs illustrate cultural influences on the structuring of early mother - child relationships.

Benedict's (1946) configurational approach is applied on the Japanese character especially the alleged influence of severe toilet training.

Child-rearing practices have, to do not only with weaning and toilet training which are relevant to adult character, but also with the influence of sleeping patterns on child development (Whittings: 1960).

Other studies deal with aspects of interdependence mainly the socialization or aggression and self-assertion, the nature of the internationalization of moral percepts, and processes of identification within the culture.

Whiting and Whiting (1960) summarizes much of these studies. While other can be found in Levine, (1960) Bacon, Child and Barry, (1959) 1963). Kiev (1960) and Kohlberg (1963).

6 ROLE EXPECTATION

Ruth Benedict's (1934) concept of configuration preceded the concept of social role (Linton, 1936) along with that of value orientation.

However the notion of culture as a patterned continuity of some sort of static totally integrated whole is implicitly in some cases explicitly questioned by a number of writers Levinson (1959) Spiro (1961) H. Philips (1963) and Inkeles (1960). These have found it more expedient to examine the interplay of social role patterns than to seek out key value orientations.

Spiro points out that roles must be prescribed since the person must perform certain acts in order to participate in a given social system. Therefore roles are determined by factors extravenious to individual inclinations.

Social systems nevertheless, motivate people to perform roles by providing inducements that can be satisfied. Despite the psychic strain individuals may undergo to make role behaviour possible in spite of negative inclinations on the part of the individual (H. Phillips: 1963).

7 VALUE ORIENTATION

In any expected role behaviour there is some form of value orientation. Therefore both the concern with social role expectation and the concern with the direct force of values as determinative influences in shaping cultural behaviour.

The current studies of value orientations seem to be a continuation of the configurational approach. These aim at a definition of "tone" (Zeitgeist) the world view (Weltanschauung) or the **"ethos"** of a culture. The use of Rorschach test inferences by Honingmann (1949) resulted in sketch of general value orientations embedded in personality.

Benedict (1953) also attempt her theory on the concept of value. Kluckhohn (1953) on the country worked with the assumption of a limited number of fundamental human problems faced by all people in all places: thereby isolating five value orientations ordering human bahaviour, cultures view of human nature, its view of the humankind relationship to nature: the valuation and ordering of time; the idealized personality type and the dominant modalities in the human relationship with other humans.

After Caudill and Scarr (1962) and Opler (1945) and Kluckhohn-Strootbeck, (1961) the new trend stresses on the importance of discontinuities in socialization experience which leads to neurotic impasses and also acculturative situations.

8 RELIGIOUS PERSPECTIVES

A review of the theoretical orientation of `psychological anthropology or approaches to culture and personality in the light of socialization process raise to us the questions of human survival and interdependence.

Survival:- That is the role of culture in human personality and the implication to the meaning of the experience of everyday living. Human experience involves the gratification of wishes, feeling of needs and deprivation. This involves the fulfillment of expectation of every living experience.

While the experience of human life is mainly of a practical utilitarian kind, the meaning of human life and survival implies a religious perspective. The normal pattern of human action needs the religious factor so as to function with less strain.

At the same time the abnormal pattern signifies the need of the religious factor in that here human expectations are doomed to frustration despite the investments of emotion placed in them.

The idea of the survival of the organism suggest that the human personality is continuously under the threat of death. Every effort for survival is in one way or the other an avoidance of death or its acceleration, since in reality it is due to come in the human life.

Even when we think of life itself, in utilitarian terms the frustrations and the threat of the unexpected is ever present.

The everyday world where the humanity struggles for survival continuously seeks to satisfy the needs for food, clothing and shelter and fights the enemies of disease, ignorance and poverty under the apparent chaos and flux of sensory experience.

Thus, the meaning of religion or the structures of belief becomes not only as a mere comfort or useful function to rescue people from isolation and alienation; but a science for survival with the power not only mandatory in social sense, but explanatory in a material one, the basis for rational behavior and a means of apprehending reality.

Clifford Geertz (1965) defines religion as a "system of symbols which acts to establish powerful, pervasive and long-lasting models and motivations in men by formulation conceptions of a general order of existence and clothing these conceptions with such an aura of factuality that the moods and motivations seem uniquely realistic. According to this view belief in religion or its symbols is an adoption of culture's model of understanding reality and an embarrassment of the proper standard of social behavior.

Religion in this context stands not only for an apprehension of reality across the whole field of life but also beyond the confines of established order. Seen this way religion "maps the connections between space and time" which are the basic aspects of the world (Levi-Strauss, 1966).

The integration of human experience in a cultural system brings emotional adjustment to expectations of others. Parsons (1952) concludes that both expectations of gratification and moral standards vary from society to society.

This fundamental fact of discrepancy seems to be constant, grounded in the nature of human personality, society and culture and their relations to each other.

9 INTERDEPENDENCE AND SURVIVAL

It is generally accepted that for human survival, the personality has to depend on others. What parsons (1952) calls tragedy or the essence of human situation cannot be faced alone. This suggest the necessity of others or of a culture, in which the frustrations of human existence can be met.

The religious perspective constitutes mechanism of adjustment to the situation of strain - that is the human experience of everyday living.

The unpredictable character of human conduct demands an emotional (also not less rational) way of acting and responding to such situations. The uncertainty that brings a constant threat of failure can be seen in all human endeavors, despite socialization process in which cultural values are embodied into the personality.

This suggests that we examine the religious perspectives in our expressive symbols and values that define the world, express feelings and help in decision making, and also help us in the process of meaning and interpretation of experience and guidance of action.

Our action (behavior) takes place in the form of social structure or an ongoing process of interaction. This demand a logico-meaning for reality in our cultural context.

10 CONCLUSION AND DISCUSSIONS

The religious perspectives in psychological anthropology are embodied in the nature of its subject matter - the culture and personality. These are not only symbolic, but also cognitive, not only emotional but also rational. They are based on the human situation itself and the nature of human life in particular.

In this paper the concept of culture was examined in terms of extreme evolutionary theoretical emphasis. However, other theoretical perspectives were examined.

The concept of personality was examined next from more or less a social psychological emphasis.

The socialization process then was examined in terms of the research areas mainly being conducted, this does not exclude an examination of the development in the past period.

In conclusion the religious perspectives are brought ought it a discussion of the issues of human survival of interdependent. Since this book was meant to examine the usefulness of `Psychological Anthropology' to the study of the Religious Phenomena or Perspective. It has done that by examining areas that fruitful research and theoretical considerations can be done.

Therefore it is concluded that:-

(1) Psychological Anthropology-approaches to culture and personality have Religious Perspectives in which theoretical considerations are necessary.

(2) Psychological Anthropology-research especially the area of socialization process can be useful in the study of religious phenomena.

10 REFERENCES

Barry, H.H., Margaret K. Bacon, and I.L. Child (1957), A Cross-cultural survey of some sex differences in socialization; Journal of Abnormal Social Psychology `55 327-332.

_____ (1959). Relations of child training to subsistence economy. American Anthropologists `61, 51-63.

Bateson, G. and Margaret Mead (1942), Balinese Character a Photographic analysis, New York, New York Academy of Science.

Beals, Ralph L. and Harry Hoijer (1953). An Introduction to Anthropology, New York, The MacMillen Co.

Benedict, Ruth (1934). Patterns of Culture, Boston New York Houghton, Mifflin Co.

Boas, Franz (1929). Anthropology and modern life, New York W.W. Norton and Co. Inc.

Boyer, Ruth M. (1964). Matrilocal family among the Mescalero: Additional data. American Anthropologist 1966, 593602.

Cohen, Y. (1955). Adolescent conflict in a Jamaican Community, Journal of Indian Psychoanalytic Institute, 9, 139-172.

Durkheim, Emile, (1938). The rules of Sociological Method, George E.G. Catlin (ed.) Chicago, the University Press.

Frazier, E. Franklin (1940). Negro Youth at the crossways: their personality development in the middle states, Washington D.C. American Council on Education.

Geertz, Clifford (1965). "Religion as a Cultural System" in Michale Baton (ed.) Anthropological Approaches to Religion, Association of social Anthropologists Monographs. No. 3) New York Fredrick A. Prager Inc., 1966.

Gulkman, M. (1954). Rituals of Rebellion in South-East Africa: the Frazer Lecture 1952 Manchester University Press.

Hollowel, A. Irving (1945). Socio-psychological Aspects of Acculturation. In the Science of Man in World Crisis, Ralph Linton (ed.) N. York Columbia University Press.

Inkels A. (1960). Industrial man: The relation of status to experience, perception and valve, American Journal of Sociology 66, 1-31.

Keesing, I, Felix M., (1958). Cultural Anthropology, New York, Rinehart and Co., Inc.

Kiev, A. (1960). Primitive therapy: A cross-cultural study of the relationship between child training and therapeutic practices related to illness. In W. Muenster Berger and S. Axelrod (Eds.) Psychoanalytic Study of Society. Vol. I New York, View Press.

Kluckhohn, Florence, R.F.L. Strobeck (1961), Varieties in valve orientations, Evanston Ill. Row and Paterson.

Kluckhohn, Clyde and Wm H. Keely (1945), the concept of culture In the Science of man in the world crisis, Ralph Linton (eds.) New York Columbia Univ. Press.

Kohlberg, L. Moral Development and Identification In H.W. Stevenson (ed.) Childhood Psychology. Yearbook of National Society for the study of Education Part I, pp. 277. 332.

Kroeber, A.L. (1952). Clyde Kluckhohn, Culture a Critical Review of Concepts and definition's Papers of the Peabody Museum of American Archaeology and Ethnology, Howard University.

Levine, R.A., (1960). The Internationalization of Political Values in Stateless Societies, Human Organization, 19, pp. 51-58.

ABOUT THE AUTHOR

The Revd. Prof. Dr. Nehemy Ndirangu Kihara was born in Nanyuki in Laikipia County of Kenya, East Africa.

He was educated at Timau in Meru County and Nairobi before graduating with a Licentiate of Theological Education from St. Paul's University (United Theological College), Limuru in Kiambu County.

He holds a Bachelor of Theology (B.Th.) in Biblical Literature and Geographic History from Christian International College.

He graduated with honors and attained a Master of Divinity (M.Div.) in Social Ethics, Psychology of Religion and Counseling, from the Interdenominational Theological Center at the Clark Atlanta University Complex.

He also attained a Doctor of Philosophy (Ph.D.) in Anthropology, Sociology of Religion and Political Science from Emory University.

As an Investigative Journalist and Radio Broadcaster this Independent Publisher hosted a weekend English and still hosts a weekly Swahili Community Show for Sagal Radio Services at WATB 1420 AM Station in Decatur, GA.

As an Interdisplinary Educator he taught Security Management and Police Studies for the Institute of Peace and Security Studies, (now known as the Department of Security and Correctional Science) of Kenyatta University in Nanyuki Campus, where he was the Coordinator of Humanities and Examinations Officer.

The Author also taught Introductory Psychology, Sociology, Criminal Procedure and Law of Evidence, Intelligence-Led Policing, Public Administration and General Management Principles among other units at the Nyeri and Embu Campuses.

He was an Adjunct Professor of Sociology/ Social Sciences at the Atlanta Campus of Saint Leo University, Tampa, Fl. Taught such courses as Anthropology, Sociology, and Criminal Justice units as Social Theory, Drugs and Society, Marriage and Family, Research Methods, Human Behavior, among others He was an Adjunct Professor of Ethics at the Georgia Campus (Henry Medical Center) of the College of Health, University of St. Francis, Joliet, Ill.,

The Author was also the founding Moderating Bishop of the Ujamaa Nomadic Church -Without Borders, as a new church- mission initiative in US. He had also been an Urban Renewal/ Organizing Pastor of Beth Salem United Presbyterian Church, Columbus, Georgia. He served as an International Missionary in California, Iowa and New York, under the Mission to US program of the Presbyterian Church, USA.

As a Senior Lecturer at Kenyatta University, the Author taught African Culture, Belief Systems, Social Theory and Research Methods units in the Department of Philosophy and Religious Studies and also in the Department of Sociology. He was also an Activist Educator, who fought for academic freedom and excellence, which led to his unfair dismissal by the government which controlled the public universities and educational institutions.

Reverend Professor Ndirangu Kihara started his career a high school teacher and principal at Muthithi Secondary School, and then an ordained Church Minister of Muthithi Parish and the Stated Clerk of the wider Murang'a Presbytery of the Presbyterian Church of East Africa.

NEHEMY N. KIHARA

BLUERGREEN PUBLISHERS

www.ingramcontent.com/pod-product-compliance
Lightning Source LLC
Chambersburg PA
CBHW070228290526
45789CB00004B/1536